One Night in the Coral Sea

Sneed B. Collard III

Illustrated by Robin Brickman

ini Charlesbridge

In late spring, a few days after the full moon, the sun sets over the Coral Sea. On Australia's Great Barrier Reef, a parrotfish finds a coral crevice to sleep in. A blue-ringed octopus creeps along the reef bottom looking for a lobster or crab to eat. A moray eel sneaks out of its den to hunt.

On this night, though, something especially remarkable is about to happen. Something that happens only once each year. It won't be long now. . . .

moray eel

2

blue-ringed octopus

A greensnout parrotfish surrounds itself with a mucus sac and beds down for the night.

Australia's Great Barrier Reef is the world's largest coral reef. It's not actually a single reef, but a collection of more than 2,800 different reefs. Each has its own shape, size, and structure. Together these reefs stretch more than 1,200 miles along Australia's east coast—the same distance as the entire west coast of the United States. Who built this incredible construction?

Animals called **corals**.

4

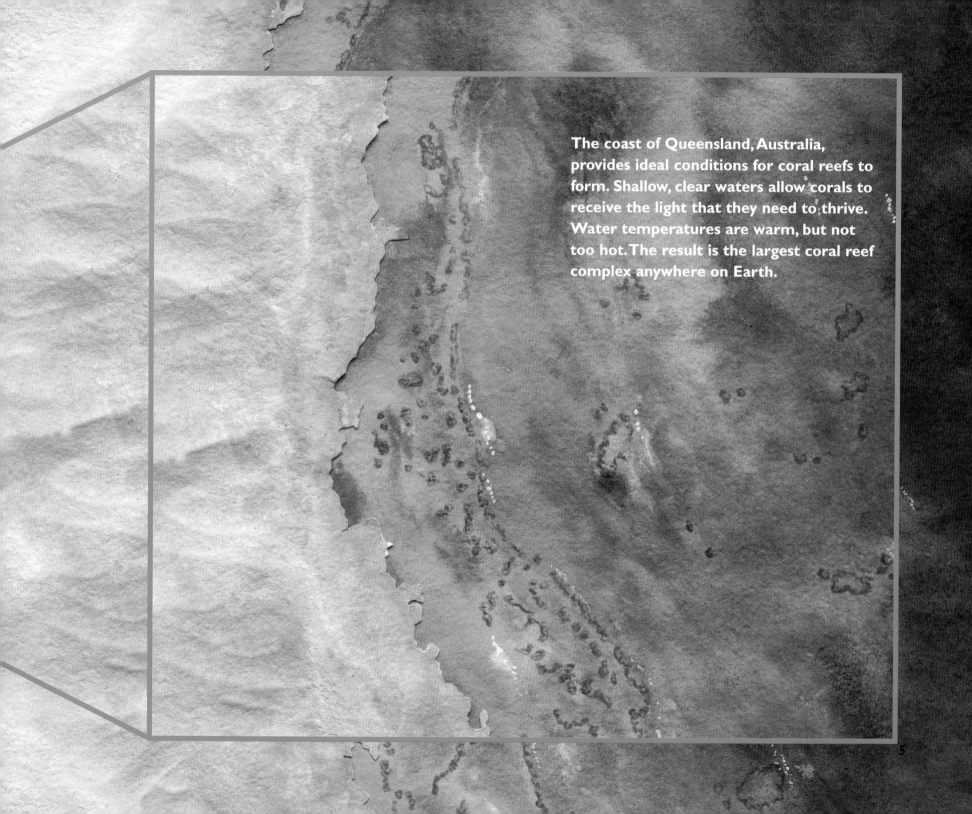

The coast of Queensland, Australia, provides ideal conditions for coral reefs to form. Shallow, clear waters allow corals to receive the light that they need to thrive. Water temperatures are warm, but not too hot. The result is the largest coral reef complex anywhere on Earth.

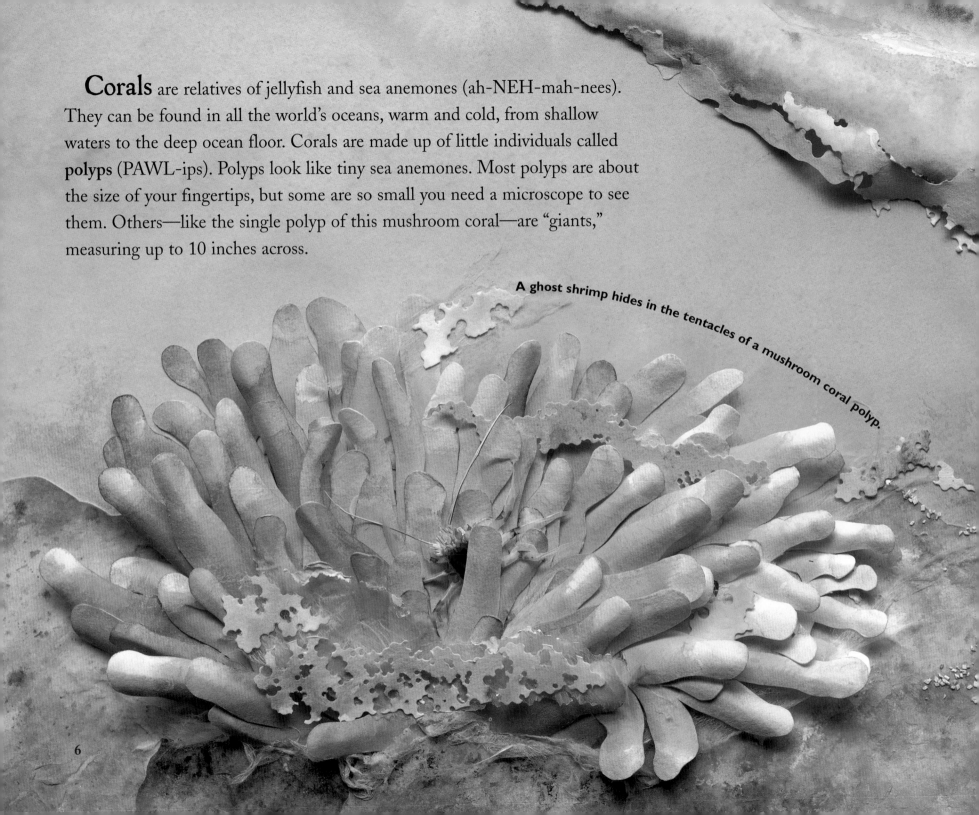

Corals are relatives of jellyfish and sea anemones (ah-NEH-mah-nees). They can be found in all the world's oceans, warm and cold, from shallow waters to the deep ocean floor. Corals are made up of little individuals called **polyps** (PAWL-ips). Polyps look like tiny sea anemones. Most polyps are about the size of your fingertips, but some are so small you need a microscope to see them. Others—like the single polyp of this mushroom coral—are "giants," measuring up to 10 inches across.

A ghost shrimp hides in the tentacles of a mushroom coral polyp.

6

Polyps have tubelike bodies where they digest their food and carry out other bodily functions. Each polyp also has a mouth surrounded by stinging tentacles that catch and kill tiny prey.

Some coral polyps live by themselves. But many coral **species** have polyps that live connected together in **colonies**. They share food with neighboring polyps and protect each other with their stinging tentacles. The coral colony grows when polyps divide in two or create new polyps through a process called **budding**.

Baby green sea turtles swim among fire coral.

A scarlet sea fan (a soft coral) beautifully camouflages a harlequin ghost pipefish.

As they grow, the polyps build skeletons for support. **Soft corals** are colonies that have soft, spongy skeletons. They include sea whips and fan corals. Soft corals are beautiful to look at, but they do not help build the reef. The reef builders belong to a second group of corals called **hard corals**.

Hard corals live only in shallow, warm tropical waters. Here their polyps lay down hard, bony skeletons made of **calcium carbonate**, also called limestone. These skeletons provide the polyps with homes and protection. They also give a reef its beautiful, amazing structure. Some hard coral colonies look like tables or shelves. Can you guess which corals are called staghorn corals and brain corals?

When a coral dies, new corals grow on top of it. Special kinds of **algae** (AL-gee) help cement the dead pieces of corals together. Over hundreds and thousands of years, large reefs form, including the world's most remarkable reef, the Great Barrier Reef.

bottlenosed dolphins

staghorn coral (a hard coral)

A school of anthias fish gather around a brain coral (a hard coral).

9

More than 340 different kinds, or species, of corals live on the Great Barrier Reef. The reef also provides a home for thousands of other animals.

Six of the world's seven species of sea turtles live on the Great Barrier Reef. So do porpoises and manatee-like animals called **dugongs**. Whales visit the reef's warm tropical waters to mate and give birth.

humpback whale and calf

a school of anthias fish

harlequin tuskfish

spott seaho

yellowmask angelfish

bryozoan

giant clam

biscuit sea star

A green sea turtle swims by corals swarming with fish.

10

More than 2,200 species of fish call the Great Barrier Reef home. They range in size from tiny gobies that hide in the corals to six-feet-long potato cod that hunt for other fish. See that whitetip reef shark and funny-looking striped boxfish? They are common reef residents.

Among the corals, you'll also discover thousands of species of **invertebrates**—animals without backbones. They include tube worms, starfish, crabs, sea cucumbers, sponges, the corals themselves, and **crinoids** (KRY-noyds)—unusual animals related to starfish.

slate-pencil sea urchin

blackback butterflyfish

anthias

damselfish

whitetip reef shark

brittlestar

striped boxfish

nudibranch
(NEW-di-brank)
"sea slug"

galaxy coral

goby

11

female squarespot anthias

male squarespot anthias

anthias

Coral reef creatures are among the most dazzling on earth. Parrotfish, butterflyfish, angelfish, and hundreds of kinds of wrasses look like they've been dipped in rainbows. Crinoids, corals, and other invertebrates are also splashed with color. These bright colors aren't just for show. Colors help reef animals attract mates, identify their own species, and—in the case of sea slugs and sea snakes—warn predators that they are poisonous.

slingjaw wrasse

blue-girdled angelfish

feather star (a kind of crinoid)

juvenile axilspot hogfish

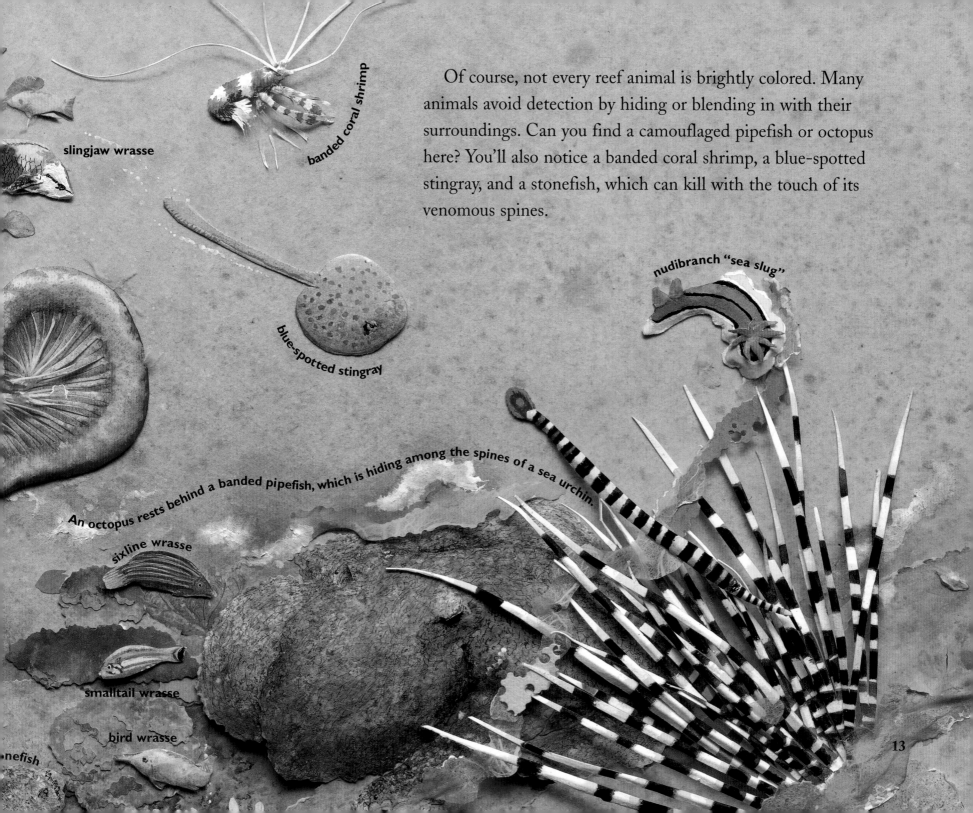

slingjaw wrasse

banded coral shrimp

Of course, not every reef animal is brightly colored. Many animals avoid detection by hiding or blending in with their surroundings. Can you find a camouflaged pipefish or octopus here? You'll also notice a banded coral shrimp, a blue-spotted stingray, and a stonefish, which can kill with the touch of its venomous spines.

nudibranch "sea slug"

blue-spotted stingray

An octopus rests behind a banded pipefish, which is hiding among the spines of a sea urchin.

sixline wrasse

smalltail wrasse

bird wrasse

nefish

orange cup coral

finger coral

scroll coral

With so many animals around, activity on the reef never stops, day or night. Almost anywhere you look, predators hunt for food while prey animals avoid becoming food. You can see animals mating, giving birth, growing, moving—there's always something amazing going on.

But one night every spring, the corals join in one of earth's most incredible spectacles. Scientists call it the **coral mass spawning** event.

soft coral

branching staghorn coral

star coral

14

The mass spawning event occurs in late spring, a few days after the full moon. As the sun sinks toward the horizon and the reef's daytime colors fade into a blue, watery dusk, the coral polyps begin to feed as they do every night. Their tentacles open to catch **plankton**—tiny animals and plants that float in the water.

But on this one night, something else starts to happen. Inside each coral polyp, tiny round spheres that look like pink, orange, or beige pebbles push up toward the polyp's mouth. Each sphere is a precious packet of eggs. The polyps bulge. Then, suddenly . . .

purple tipped coral

pineapple coral

star coral

15

A polyp pops open! Its egg packets escape and float like balloons up toward the sea surface. All around, other polyps also open, releasing their egg packets.

As soon as the polyps from one coral colony begin to release their egg packets, others follow. In no time, dozens of species of corals begin releasing their egg packets. Together the spawning corals release hundreds of egg packets. Thousands of them . . .

pineapple coral

Millions . . . Trillions.

Each coral egg packet can contain dozens or even hundreds of eggs. As the packets float upward, they split open and the eggs separate and float on their own.

Along with the eggs, the corals release trillions of tiny sperm. Many sperm are carried in the same packets as the eggs. Others are released in milky clouds directly into the sea. Once a sperm is free, it wriggles through the water, searching for an egg from its own species of coral. This is not an easy task!

various butterflyfish species feeding on coral eggs

mushroom corals releasing sperm (this is a different kind of mushroom coral from page 6)

18

During the mass spawning, more than 135 species of corals may release their eggs and sperm at the same time. Scientists believe that special substances on an egg's surface allow a sperm to recognize its own kind of egg.

When a sperm does find an egg from its own species, it attaches to it. Hundreds of other sperm also arrive, all of them pushing to penetrate the egg's thin, soft surface. As soon as one sperm enters an egg, the egg "locks out" all the other sperm. Then the contents of the sperm and egg join together. This joining is called **fertilization**.

With fertilization, a new life begins.

fertilization magnified

By morning huge slicks of eggs and sperm cover the Coral Sea surface. For the eggs that have been fertilized, their journey is just beginning.

A fertilized egg divides into two cells, then four, then eight, and a tiny coral begins to form. This coral doesn't look anything like its parents. As its cells divide and grow, it becomes a **planula larva** (PLAN-you-la LAR-vuh). The larva has hairlike **cilia** (SILL-ee-uh) that beat through the water, allowing the larva to swim.

Portuguese man-of-war

A fertilized coral egg divides and divides again and a coral larva grows.

princess damselfish

The **larvae** (LAR-vee) are not strong swimmers. They mostly drift on the ocean currents flowing through the Coral Sea. They float in these currents for days, sometimes weeks. They swirl around and are carried dozens, even hundreds, of miles.

Unlucky larvae are eaten by fish or jellyfish. Others are carried far from the reef or washed up on shore, where they perish. However, there are so many larvae that many survive.

Günther's wrasse

lemon damselfish

The lucky larvae escape predators and float on currents close to a reef. After a week or so, these larvae sink toward the bottom. Swimming with their tiny cilia, the larvae search for a good place to live. How do they know where to settle? Scientists believe that the larvae are attracted to chemicals released by algae on the reefs. These algae grow in well-lit, favorable places.

Settling in a well-lit place is important because corals have life forms called **zooxanthellae** (ZOE-zan-THEL-ee) living inside them. Zooxanthellae use sunlight to make food and share that food with the coral colony. This process is an example of **symbiosis.** Coral polyps still catch their own food, but zooxanthellae allow corals to grow fast enough and big enough to build reefs.

After finding a good spot, each larva cements itself in place and goes through a **metamorphosis** (MET-uh-MOR-foe-sis), just like a caterpillar. Instead of turning into a butterfly, though, the larva turns into a tiny coral polyp.

planula (magnified)

Zooxanthellae, the tiny specks seen here on this frogspawn coral, can only be seen under a mi

diagonal-banded sweetlips

staghorn coral

close-up of a coral larva finding a new home on the reef

23

Over time the new polyp feeds and grows larger. Soon it buds or divides to make more polyps.

scroll coral

lionfish

24

sea fan

And more . . .

Damselfish and lionfish find shelter among the growing coral. Tube worms and shrimp burrow into the coral, and even a giant clam starts to grow. Butterflyfish, cone snails, and starfish eat some of the coral, but through it all, the coral keeps growing.

crown-of-thorns starfish

giant clam

blue sea star

cone snail

two juvenile gray demoiselle

25

As the years pass, the coral blossoms into a full colony. It becomes an important part of the reef, just like the corals that gave birth to it.

Coral reefs below the sea surface prepare for a mass spawning event.

Then, one evening, a few days after a full moon in spring, the coral joins millions of other corals. As the sun falls in the Southern Hemisphere and stars scatter like sand over the sky, the coral prepares for its own first mass spawning event. . . .

27

One night in the Coral Sea.

28

More About Coral Mass Spawning

This book describes one of nature's most amazing spectacles. Until the 1980s, no one even knew that it happened. Then, in 1984, scientists on Australia's Great Barrier Reef discovered that dozens of the reef's coral species **spawned**, or released their eggs and sperm, all at the same time.

After that discovery, researchers found other mass spawnings on coral reefs in other parts of the world. However, scientists found that only on the Great Barrier Reef and other reefs in the Indo-Pacific region did such a large number of coral species spawn together. On the Great Barrier Reef more than 135 of the reef's 340 species of corals join in mass spawnings.

Spawning helps corals in a number of ways. Since adult corals can't move, spawning allows them to spread their young over wide areas and expand their range. However, mass spawning has an additional advantage. With so many corals releasing their eggs at one time, predators can eat only a small percentage of them before they get full. Fish and other predators leave most of the eggs to float on their merry way, increasing the eggs' chances of establishing new coral colonies. Without this remarkable event many coral species may not have survived for so long or been able to build the incredible reefs we enjoy today.

As scientists continue to study mass spawning, they will learn more about this amazing event. Their discoveries will also help us understand and protect one of our planet's most awesome natural wonders, the Great Barrier Reef.

To Find Out More About Corals

BOOKS

Arnold, Caroline. *A Walk on the Great Barrier Reef.* Minneapolis, MN: Carolrhoda Books, 1988.

Cerullo, Mary M. *Coral Reef: A City That Never Sleeps.* New York, NY: Cobblehill Books/Dutton, 1996.

Collard, Sneed B. III. *Our Wet World: Exploring Earth's Aquatic Ecosystems.* Watertown, MA: Charlesbridge, 1998.

Collard, Sneed B. III. *Lizard Island: Science and Scientists on Australia's Great Barrier Reef.* Danbury, CT: Franklin Watts, 2000.

Muzik, Kathy. *At Home in the Coral Reef.* Watertown, MA: Charlesbridge, 1992.

Pringle, Laurence. *Coral Reefs: Earth's Undersea Treasures.* New York, NY: Simon & Schuster, 1995.

WEBSITES (please note that web addresses change)

www.gbrmpa.gov.au
This site of the Great Barrier Reef Marine Park Authority provides information and links that will answer just about any question you have about Great Barrier Reef.

www.coralreefalliance.org
The Coral Reef Alliance is a group that is working to stop the worldwide destruction of coral reefs. This site features news items pertaining to coral reefs, offers information about ongoing coral programs, and provides links to many other useful sites.

www.epa.gov/OWOW/oceans/coral/
The U. S. Environmental Protection Agency devoted this website to coral reefs. It includes general information about reefs, current activities to protect them, and links to other sites and information.

Glossary

Algae: Plants that live in water, such as oceans and lakes. Note: Not all aquatic plants are algae—sea grasses, for example are not.

Bud: A new individual that develops asexually from an adult animal such as a sea anemone or coral. Buds may later separate from their "parent" or become part of a parent's colony.

Budding: A method corals use to reproduce whereby a piece, or bud, from the parent grows to form a new polyp.

Calcium carbonate: The hard, bonelike material made by reef-building corals, which they then use to make their skeletons. Also called "limestone."

Cilia: Tiny hairlike structures that are used by many larvae and plankton for swimming or feeding.

Coral colonies: Coral polyps that are connected together by their tissues and have a common skeleton for support.

Coral mass spawning event: When many polyps from different coral colonies and species release their eggs and sperm into the water at the same time. Also called "synchronous spawning."

Corals: An individual polyp or colony of polyps, including their skeletons. Corals are related to jellyfish and sea anemones, and most corals have stinging tentacles.

Crinoids: An ancient group of animals related to sea stars, or "starfish." Many grow fixed in place, while others can move. They filter small animals and other food out of the water. Includes sea lilies and feather stars.

Dugongs: Marine mammals related to manatees. Unlike manatees, which can often be found in rivers, dugongs live only in the ocean. They graze on shallow sea grasses.

Fertilization: The process in which a sperm and egg join together to form a new living organism, such as a planula larva.

Hard corals: Coral colonies that build hard, bony skeletons made of calcium carbonate or "limestone." Also called "reef-building corals."

Invertebrates: Animals that do not have backbones. Corals are invertebrates.

Larvae: More than one larva.

Metamorphosis: The process in which a larva changes into another form or shape. A planula larva, for instance, goes through metamorphosis to become a coral polyp.

Plankton: Small plants and animals of various species that drift on currents due to their limited ability to swim.

Planula larva or "planula": An oblong, early stage of a coral. The larva looks much different than its parent.

Polyps: A polyp is the body of an individual coral. Each polyp has a tubular body and a mouth surrounded by tentacles. In coral colonies, polyps are connected together and share food.

Soft corals: Coral colonies that build soft, flexible skeletons. Sea whips and sea fans are kinds of soft corals.

Spawn: Animals, such as corals, spawn by releasing eggs and sperm into the water so that fertilization can take place.

Species: A group of similar animals, plants, or other organisms that share common traits. An individual of a species usually can reproduce only with another individual of that same species. For instance, a dugong can only reproduce with another dugong.

Symbiosis: A close relationship between two different species that benefits each other in some way, such as the relationship between reef-building corals and zooxanthellae.

Zooxanthellae: Tiny life forms that live within corals and other organisms. Like plants, they use the sun's energy to make food. Zooxanthellae share this food with corals or other host animals.

Index

For my Aunts, DD, Linda, and Mary Anne—
three of the most colorful creatures I know.
        Love, Sneed

For Mathias Jessup Bartels—a much-loved boy and a wonder of nature
        —R. B.

On the front cover: yellowstripe anthias, blackback butterflyfish, yellow boxfish, and pineapple coral
On the front flap: blue-ringed octopus
On title page: squirrelfish with feather star coral
On the back cover: many-lined sweetlips, baby green sea turtle, and pineapple coral

Acknowledgments:

The author wishes to thank the many scientists and managers working at the Lizard Island Research Station for helping me share the magic of the Great Barrier Reef and the coral mass spawning event. Special thanks to Anne Hoggett, Lyle Vail, Andrew Heyward, and Andrew Negri.

Published by Charlesbridge
85 Main Street
Watertown, MA 02472
(617) 926-0329
www.charlesbridge.com

Library of Congress Cataloging-in-Publication Data
Collard, Sneed B.
   One night in the Coral Sea / Sneed B. Collard III ; illustrated by Robin Brickman.
     p. cm.
   ISBN 1-57091-389-7 (reinforced for library use)
1. Corals—Australia—Great Barrier Reef (Qld.)—Juvenile literature. 2. Coral reef animals—Australia—Great Barrier Reef (Qld.)—Juvenile literature. I. Brickman, Robin, ill. II. Title.
QL377.C5C65 2005
593.6—dc22   2004003307

Printed in Thailand
(hc) 10 9 8 7 6 5 4 3 2 1

Three-dimensional illustrations made of paper painted and sculpted by Robin Brickman
Display type set in P22 Mayflower and text type set in Adobe Caslon
Art photographed by Gamma One
Color separated, printed, and bound by Imago
Production supervision by Brian G. Walker; designed by Susan M. Sherman